Original title:
Life's Puzzle: Still Looking for the Edges

Copyright © 2025 Creative Arts Management OÜ
All rights reserved.

Author: Lucas Harrington
ISBN HARDBACK: 978-1-80566-273-0
ISBN PAPERBACK: 978-1-80566-568-7

Mapping the Invisible

With crayons in hand, I draw my fate,
Colors collide, but oh, they wait.
A treasure map to hidden delight,
X marks the spot? Nope, that's just my kite.

In the forest of doubts, I wander free,
Chasing shadows, where could they be?
The compass spins like a joke on me,
North, south, or upside down? Who could see?

Staying Open to Possibility

A door ajar with a squeak and a sigh,
What's in there? A dragon? A pie?
I tiptoe in with a grin on my face,
Might find a circus or a magic place.

Jumping on clouds like they're trampolines,
Bouncing between all my wild daydreams.
Do I land softly or crash, who can tell?
I'll laugh it off, guess I'm under a spell!

The Space Between Whys

Why does my sock always disappear?
Is it a thief or a cloth-footed seer?
In the abyss of laundry, I cry and pout,
Where's it gone? I've got my doubts!

Asking questions like a curious cat,
Wondering where the lost things sat.
In the gaps between answers I smile,
Because the mystery's worth it, at least for a while!

Patterns in the Disarray

My room looks like a tornado just danced,
A pile of clothes that fate has chanced.
Searching for order in chaos that reigns,
Maybe I'll find it in the fish pulled from trains.

Socks with stripes and shirts made of spots,
In this mix-up, I'm tying the knots.
Who needs a pattern when fun's in a twist?
Just call me the jester, it's all in the mist!

Navigating Shadows and Light

In a room full of socks, I play hide and seek,
The left one's a rebel, it's never meek.
Under the couch, I find a lone shoe,
Turns out it's a portal! Who knew?

Juggling my keys while looking for clues,
The cat has the map, but she won't share the views.
A flashlight in hand, I venture to inspect,
But the ghost of my snacks is what I detect.

In Search of the Missing Link

My brain is a jigsaw with pieces misplaced,
Should I be a genius or simply outpaced?
Recalling the puzzle, I scratch my head,
Is that breakfast's bagel or thoughts of dread?

Searching for meaning in the bottom of my cup,
Caffeine conspiracies, oh, will I erupt?
Each sip brings a giggle, a snicker, a laugh,
Maybe the answer's just my other half.

The Colors of Uncertainty

Paint swirls around, like a wild little dance,
Accidental art? Oh, what a chance!
I spilled my ideas on the canvas today,
If only my focus wouldn't run away!

Crayons and markers in a colorful mess,
Drawing a map for my motivated stress.
Why is the sunshine wearing polka dots?
And what's with the purple on all the hot pots?

Shards of Memory

Rumors of my youth are all in the air,
Did I ride a dinosaur? Or just comb my hair?
Every fragment's a riddle, a laugh or a tear,
A dance around the turkey, a really loud cheer.

One shard's a cat, who swears he can sing,
While another's a snail that lost his bling.
Slicing through moments, I add a new box,
Watch out for the time that squawks, then rocks!

Patterns of Everyday Wonder

In the morning, socks elope,
One goes green, the other a dope.
Cereal dances in the bowl,
Milk does a twirl, what a roll!

Cats play chess with the old dog,
Who wins? It's just a fog!
Sun shines bright, but who will care?
Forget the game, let's raise a chair!

Pants on backwards? That's my style,
With a shirt too big, what a trial!
Spilled my coffee, it's a sight,
Laugh it off, everything's alright!

Every day brings something new,
A quirky glitch, an odd viewpoint.
So we giggle through the fray,
Embrace the strange, let's start the play!

The Underlying Design

Jigsaw pieces hide and seek,
They giggle softly, then they sneak.
One's a cat, another a shoe,
This odd shape? Oh, that must be you!

Puzzles mixed, the colors collide,
A rainbow throws a wild ride.
Corners missing, edges blur,
But laugh with me, let's not deter!

Spilled the beans on the dinner plate,
Mismatched cutlery seals the fate.
Grandma's soup, like a work of art,
How did we get here? A mystery start!

Take a chance with every bite,
Who cares if it's wrong or right?
Finding humor in the mess,
Embracing chaos, nothing less!

Reaching for the Unattainable

I climbed a tree, stretched my arms,
But reached for clouds, not charms.
Fell into a pile of leaves,
Looked like I lost all my keys!

Stars above are slyly winks,
While I'm stuck, pondering drinks.
Can't catch a dream, it flits away,
Doing the dance of 'What to say?'

Driving circles just to park,
Life's a riddle, let's leave a mark.
The cookie jar is out of reach,
Let's plot, my friend; it's time to breach!

So tiptoe through the crazy plot,
Chasing after what we've got.
With laughter, joy, and silly schemes,
We'll catch those stars, or so it seems!

The Search for Synergy

Two left feet try to dance,
Tripping over every chance.
Rhythms clash, a wild show,
But hey, at least we're on the go!

Mixing flavors in a stew,
Beating eggs, two and two.
Burnt a dish? Never fear,
We'll still laugh and grab a beer!

Colors clash on the canvas bright,
Yet somehow, it feels just right.
Blob of paint, a dance of cheer,
In every chaos, I see clear!

So grab your friend, let's make a mess,
Together we'll face the needless stress.
In every blunder, a tune to sing,
Finding joy in every quirky thing!

Embracing the Unknown

In a world where socks disappear,
I chase the chaos, never fear.
Flip-flops on a snowy day,
Who knew warmth would lead me astray?

I try to cook, set off the smoke,
Dinner guests just laugh and poke.
The cake I baked could barely rise,
I swear it had too many spies!

A map for life? I lost the thread,
With crumbs for guidance, I forged ahead.
Life's recipe: a dash of zest,
Oh, but the taste? A funny jest!

Trails of Discovery

In the woods, I lost my way,
Chased a squirrel, went astray.
Found a tree that looked like me,
With a knot that whispered, "Be free!"

A path of rocks and muddy shoes,
Greet the rain, I must refuse.
Dancing puddles, splashing wide,
I've got rubber boots—what a ride!

A table gets set, but all is wrong,
Spilled my drink, played the song.
With hiccups, laughter, and grins abound,
Who knew fun in messes was profound?

Reflections on the Unsought

Mirror, mirror, what do you see?
A face that looks a lot like me.
But wait, is that a cookie crumb?
I swear I cleaned up—oh, how I've come!

The shirt inside out, my hair a mess,
Fashionably late, I must confess.
In a world of trends I don't quite know,
I'm rocking confusion like a pro!

Showing up with mismatched shoes,
Strutting boldly, spreading news.
Who cares for norms? Let's twist and shout,
In the circus of life, I have no doubt!

The Continuum of Questions

Why do we park in driveways, I wonder?
And loafers, are they for bread or lumber?
Who invented the word 'abbreviation'?
A riddle wrapped in my own frustration!

If a tree falls, does it still make noise?
What's the point of all these toys?
Do fish get thirsty? I need to know,
The answers linger, and thoughts just flow!

Why do cats ignore our calls?
Do they plan world takeovers in the halls?
We live in questions, that's our fate,
In this funny world, let's celebrate!

The Quest for Unity

In a world of mismatched socks,
I search for pairs, but who has time?
A shoehorn's not the answer here,
The wardrobe's got its own mad rhyme.

I tried to bake a perfect pie,
But ended up with lava flow.
The recipe was clear as mud,
What's sweet may turn to bitter dough.

I mix my drinks with such great flair,
Yet spill it all on my best shirt.
It's fun to dance with beverage in hand,
But laundry day's a flirty flirt.

Each piece I find, it cracks me up,
The corners fit but look so weird.
Who knew the cat was part of this?
And why is he now highly cheered?

Resilience in Disarray

My socks are swirling in a dance,
A war declared on matching pairs.
They leap and twirl, a sock ballet,
While I just sit, scratched head and stares.

The toast I made has flown away,
A rogue slice launched with great intent.
It landed on the cat's fine coat,
So now, it seems, he's heaven-sent.

I tried to plant a garden bright,
But only weeds have taken hold.
I water them and they just smile,
This chaos never gets too old.

And life throws pies, some well-aimed hits,
I get a smile from every splat.
Embracing chaos, dancing through,
Is better than a perfect plat.

Courting Complexity

My planner's more a work of art,
With doodles, dreams, and snack attacks.
Schedules flipped like circus tricks,
I laugh and dance, no need to relax.

The dog has mastered hide-and-seek,
Disappearing from my sight.
I search and call, he's in the yard,
With muddy paws, he's won this fight.

I joined a gym to feel so spry,
Yet weights confuse me, much to my woe.
My aerobics turn to circus acts,
Just look at me, the fitness pro!

Yet life unfolds with sharp turns gained,
With every twist, laughter's mine.
Who needs a blueprint, stick or plan,
When wobbly comes with glasses of wine?

A Journey Through the Unsure

I ventured out to find some peace,
But stumbled on a sock brigade.
They marched around, my feet beguiled,
Who knew fashion had such a charade?

I plotted paths with maps galore,
But ended up in donut hell.
Sugar high led me astray,
Now all I do is munch and dwell.

Mistaking tools for breakfast goods,
I made a smoothie full of screws.
Blenders whirred with clangs and pops,
Now I've got drinks to make you snooze.

So here's the truth, in jumbled fun,
Embrace the twists, the slips, the cracks.
When chaos reigns, just laugh aloud,
Your journey's best with snacks and jacks.

Pieces of Tomorrow Yet to Fit

In a world of jigsaw dreams,
Where each day is what it seems,
I lost a piece under the couch,
A sock, a shoe, oh what a slouch.

Colors clash like cats and dogs,
The sun shines bright, then hides in fogs,
Balancing cups of coffee spill,
On toes, it's funny, I've got skill.

Some edges are rough, some corners bent,
Mismatched puzzles seem heaven-sent,
Each piece I find brings laughter bright,
Inquirin' where I left my light.

So here I sit, with gaps in place,
A grin upon my scruffy face,
Tomorrow's pieces yet unfit,
But isn't chaos, just a hit?

Of Mismatched Moments and Serendipity

Stumbling through the days we roam,
With mismatched socks, we call it home,
The toast burns while the coffee spills,
Such joyful chaos brings us thrills.

Tripping over yesterday's shoes,
A life of laughter, endless clues,
The clock ticks loud, misshapes the time,
Yet here we dance, to wobbly rhyme.

In every twist, there's some delight,
Like finding jellybeans at night,
We chase the giggles, dropping hints,
Of happy moments, serenely dense.

So raise a glass to all we've missed,
To awkward dances, and shouted lists,
For in this mess, we surely fit,
With joy and laughter, we are lit.

Scribbles of Hope in a Chaotic Realm

In a land of scribbles, hope's alive,
Where doodles dance and dreams arrive,
Crayons clash, a rainbow's spree,
At least they won't get lost at sea.

My adulting skills, quite off the chart,
With paper planes, I'm set to start,
Crashing often, yet taking flight,
In crayon hues, I find my light.

Scrambled plans upon the fridge,
Some days I oscillate on a ridge,
With every splatter, crazed and loud,
Hope scribbles bright, beneath the cloud.

So grab a marker, let's create,
A world where chaos feels just great,
For every mess is art's sweet kiss,
A funny tale we can't dismiss.

The Harmony of Asymmetry

In perfect chaos, find the flow,
With crooked smiles that steal the show,
Notes are played in offbeat tunes,
Dancing under careless moons.

The pie's unsliced, the cake's a mess,
Life's recipe? Just guess and guess,
Though mismatched tones create a sound,
A harmony that knows no bounds.

With laughter's echo, things align,
In wobbly shapes, we intertwine,
Finding joy in every slip,
This jester's life, a funny trip.

So let's embrace this quirky play,
With shades of weird brightening the day,
In every blunder, joy is found,
A maddening bliss that knows no bound.

Chasing Silhouettes

In the morning, I seek my socks,
Yet find only mismatched rocks.
Chasing shadows on the floor,
Where'd I put my keys once more?

Honey, where's the cat gone now?
He's hiding under the cows.
A circus of chaos, pure delight,
As I trip over lunch at night.

Each corner hides a curious tale,
Of countless quests that always fail.
I laugh and grin at every fall,
Life's a circus; I'm the clown of all.

In the end, I'll find my stride,
With grace that comes from blunders wide.
The dance of life is quite the sight,
And makes each day feel so just right.

Threads of the Unfinished

My sweater's missing a whole sleeve,
When I looked, I couldn't believe!
Threads tangled in a great big mess,
A masterpiece, I must confess.

Knitting failed but humor thrives,
As I wear my fashion jives.
Scarves that flap like hungry birds,
I call them art in simple words.

Each project left to gather dust,
In the chaos, I must trust.
A quilt of dreams, all still half-finished,
Underneath, my humor's nourished.

So here I sit, my craft a hoot,
In a world of whimsy, I'm resolute!
For laughter's thread will hold me tight,
While I weave my world in playful light.

The Great Mosaic of Being

I'm a tile in a grand design,
A bit off-color, but I'm just fine!
Each crack a story, bright and bold,
In this art, I'm worth more than gold.

With every piece that seems to clash,
Together we make a colorful splash.
Let's glue our quirks and jumbled dreams,
Life's a canvas bursting at the seams!

A jigsaw puzzle without a frame,
Where silly antics are the name of the game.
I dance crooked but still I shine,
In this crazy quilt, I'm divine!

So let's embrace the wild degree,
Of mismatched colors in harmony.
Each flaw a wink, a chuckle too,
The great mosaic is me and you.

Echoes of What Could Be

In the attic lies a dusty dream,
With echoes of a grander scheme.
A plan to bake the world a pie,
But I burnt the crust—oh me, oh my!

The recipes are written in jest,
I boil the water, forget the rest.
I'll paint the sky with shades of glee,
While my cake hopes to be free!

With every failed attempt to soar,
I laugh at clouds; I might explore.
A kite that's stuck upon the tree,
Snares my spirit endlessly.

So raise a toast to every blunder,
To echo dreams that pull us under.
For laughter's there in what we seek,
In messy moments, we're unique!

Seeking the Corner Pieces

In a box, far and wide,
Lies a jumble, we must abide.
Corners hide with a snicker,
Elusive pieces, oh, look quicker!

Cats chase shadows, dogs chase tails,
While I hunt for glossy scales.
The corners giggle, making me mad,
Yet, I can't help but feel quite glad!

Whispers in the Gaps

Where did that piece of orange go?
Lost in the madness, I can't say no!
It whispers secrets from the floor,
"Find me quick! I'm hard to ignore."

With laughter, I stumble and dive,
In search of what makes this come alive.
Each gap a mystery, each crevice a joke,
"Who needs a plan?" my inner self woke!

Finding Balance in Chaos

Balancing pieces like I balance work,
Missing corners make me berserk.
I stack them high, one on another,
"Don't fall, please!" I call to my mother.

Wobbling like a quirky tower,
Controlled chaos, I'm in power!
But a sneeze, a laugh, and oh no!
The whole thing topples, my face aglow!

The Art of Assembling Dreams

With colors bright and edges clear,
I craft a picture year by year.
Dreams like jigsaw pieces unite,
But some days, the fit just doesn't feel right.

I smile at faces, some silly, some sweet,
Each piece a memory, a little treat.
I've got the glue, for all that I lack,
Just hoping those corners don't stage a comeback!

Insights in the Intervals

In a jigsaw land where pieces stray,
My cat thinks he's the king of play,
He steals my work with purrs and flips,
While I chase tails and empty sips.

Gathering thoughts like lost puzzles,
As coffee spills turn into muzzles,
I ponder where the edges go,
Should I check under the sofa? Who knows!

Hidden Corners of Awareness

Behind the couch, a sock appears,
I hope it's not my ex's fears,
It's funny how they fade away,
Like missing pieces at a play.

A grumpy ghost of laundry fights,
Woes of unworn outfits' rights,
Yet scraps of joy in shadows blend,
What's lost may turn into a friend.

Threads of Convergence

In a world of mismatched suits,
Knitting dreams from tangled roots,
My sweater looks like a clown's delight,
Yet warmth prevails, a cozy sight.

Strings of laughter weave and bend,
Awkward moments seem to lend,
A joy in flaws that thread the seams,
Building hope from silly dreams.

The Dance of Disparate Pieces

In a quirky dance of odd ballet,
My left foot dreams of keen ballet,
While the right say, 'Let's just groove!',
We'll tango on, improve, improve!

With socks that never seem to match,
I'll still waltz in a wild dispatch,
Embracing every quirk and twist,
In laughter's sway, things can't be missed!

Puzzles of the Soul

In the box, I find a piece,
Curved the wrong way, what a tease!
I turn and twist, it fits like cheese,
Why must it be such a breeze?

The cat joins in with a sly grin,
Knocking pieces, oh where to begin?
With every step, I lose my skin,
And yet they say, it's a win-win!

I asked my friend, he's lost too,
Searching for the edge, just like you.
But all we find is a sock or shoe,
Who knew puzzles could cause such rue?

Maybe one day, we'll get it right,
With colors bright, a dazzling sight.
Until then, we make our plight,
And call it art, with all our might.

Shadows of What We Seek

In dim lit rooms, we search around,
For missing bits, not to be found.
Shadows whisper, they make no sound,
Yet here we laugh, what joy unbound!

With a magnifying glass, I squint,
Can't find the edge, not even a hint.
It's like a chase of the windprint,
Still searching for that final glint.

Should I try the fridge, who knows now?
Maybe the pieces are in a cow!
Foil-wrapped snacks, don't ask me how,
Eating 'til we solve it—oh wow!

But in the end, it's just some fun,
Building chaos, we'll never shun.
Laughter echoes, and we all run,
Because puzzles solved, are boring, hon.

Building Bridges of Hope

With tiny hands, we stack and build,
A bridge of pieces, somewhat thrilled.
Yet here I stand, a bit unfilled,
Who knew this task would be so wild?

The colors clash, a vibrant mess,
Changing norms, we'll never guess.
Here in the chaos, we find success,
A masterpiece, a sweet excess.

Forgotten wisdom in every turn,
As pieces flip, my head does burn.
But here's a tip, you'll soon discern,
It's all a joke, we laugh and learn!

We bridge the gap, with playful glee,
As laughter echoes through debris.
In every piece, we find a key,
Together here, we're wild and free.

Perspectives on the Missing Piece

So on a quest, I start to roam,
Where is the piece to call my home?
In the dog's bed? Behind the comb?
I find a jellybean... not my dome!

A wise old owl in trees does speak,
Life's a game, and I feel weak.
Every time I try to sneak,
I find another snack to peak!

Friends will help, or so they say,
Yet they sit laughing, what a play!
With every find, we dance away,
Who needs that piece? Let's have a fray!

In the chaos, we find our cheer,
Every corner stocked with beer.
Let's toast to puzzles full of fear,
'Cause funny faces bring us near!

Fragments of a Forgotten Tapestry

Once I found a sock in the drawer,
Thought it was art—an odd decor.
Each piece tells a story that's half-told,
In mismatched laundry, mysteries unfold.

The cat pounced, thinking it was a mouse,
But it was just fabric lounging in the house.
Thread by thread, I stitch the day,
In colors bright, come what may.

Old magazines lay scattered about,
Their glossy smiles give me a shout.
Are they lost treasures or just plain trash?
In this chaos, my memories clash.

So here I sit, with scissors and glue,
Creating a tale, absurd yet true.
Every snippet a laugh, every tear a cheer,
In this tapestry, nothing's austere.

The Quest for Cornerstone Moments

Searching for the moments that fit just right,
Like puzzle pieces late at night.
The cat steals a piece, with a playful heart,
Is it a game or a missing part?

In kitchens bright, I mix and stir,
Why do my cakes always prefer to blurr?
The toppings flee, the frosting slides,
In culinary arts, my confidence hides.

Chasing corners like a knight in quest,
Finding the edges is quite the test.
What's the secret to scoring a win?
In this quirky game, let the fun begin!

With friends who laugh, and snacks to share,
Every twist and turn takes us somewhere.
So let's find the corners, let's round them out,
And celebrate silliness, that's what it's about!

Whispers of the Unfinished Picture

In the attic, dust bunnies roam,
An unfinished canvas calls me home.
Brush in hand, but where's the flow?
Is this art, or just paint thrown in a show?

The sketch of a cat, or is it a bee?
The lines are tangled, who could it be?
With giggles echoing off the walls,
I scribble on—no fear of falls.

Each color a giggle, a hiccup, a snort,
This piece of chaos, a funny report.
Yet the canvas stares, demanding to know,
Will I finish it? Maybe... but oh, look at that glow!

So I dance around with my paint brushes bright,
Collecting stories from day until night.
In the whispers that linger, confusion's the call,
This unfinished picture? I'm having a ball!

Jigsaw Dreams Beneath the Surface

Puzzles sprawled across the living room floor,
Each piece giggles, begging for more.
Under the sofa, a piece does hide,
Was it shy, or just hoping to slide?

Family game night brings out the crew,
Grandma smirks like she already knew.
With laughter exploding, the pieces fly,
Who needs order? Let chaos apply!

A corner piece claimed by the dog,
Leaving confusion amidst our dialogue.
Am I missing part of my sanity too?
Or is it just the fun in the view?

As pieces mingle under the light,
We create memories—oh what a sight!
So let's dive in, feet first to the mess,
In jigsaw dreams, there's always success!

Sketches of the Unseen

In a world of mismatched socks,
I search for my lost keys,
Chasing crumbs and broken clocks,
The cat's stealing my cheese.

My coffee's always steaming hot,
Yet in my cup, there's only air,
I question if it's all a plot,
Where did my sanity wander, where?

Jigsaw pieces made of fluff,
That somehow fit just fine;
With every giggle, it's enough,
The chaos makes me shine.

A map with no designated path,
Leading me to silly sights,
With laughter echoing the math,
I'll find my way in flights.

Harmony Amongst the Hectic

In a dance of flying shoes,
My plans are like tangled hair,
I sip my drink and barely choose,
To laugh at fate's wild dare.

Meetings turn to verbal games,
With voices crossing like a net,
The coffee pot spills all the names,
Yet still, I'm not upset.

Grown-ups juggling tasks like clowns,
While kids sport sticky fingers,
Around the city, honking sounds,
A symphony that lingers.

I find a rhythm in the mess,
As laughter dances in the air,
Each misstep turns to pure finesse,
Creating joy everywhere.

Echoes of the Incomplete

Incomplete thoughts in jars align,
With Gummy bears and random toys,
Trying to figure out the sign,
That means I've grown up, no noise.

I wrote a book on how to beam,
But misplaced my dazzling stare,
Did it all happen in a dream,
Or was it just a mad affair?

My to-do list likes to grow,
While snacks conspire to distract,
With each attempt, I leap and flow,
Missing steps is how I act.

Yet laughter bursts in every crack,
A melody of mishaps bright,
In every puzzle, there's a knack,
To turn the day into pure light.

Unwritten Chapters

A blank page calls, what's in the air?
With scribbles of the silly kind,
The plot twists hover without a care,
As I grasp at what's confined.

Procrastination plays a role,
With cookies beckoning my pen,
I'd write a story, but oh, the toll,
Of treats that drag me back again!

In moments lost among the fun,
Life's verses dance atop the floor,
Though unclasped, the stories run,
From the heart, forever more.

Each laugh, a page in time's embrace,
While letters leap from my delight,
To write unwritten dreams in space,
Chasing shadows, day turns night.

Searching for the Last Piece

In the drawer, I found my stash,
Old socks and a half-eaten mash.
Puzzle pieces in a sock,
Why'd I think it'd be in the dock?

Under the couch, a treasure awaits,
Dust bunnies guard my soulmates.
They giggle and swish, full of cheer,
While I question my sanity here!

A cat walks by, pawing my quest,
With each step, I think I'm blessed.
But no piece can put me at ease,
Ah, the thrill of the patchy tease!

Maybe it's lost in space, or in time,
Like my missing socks—it's a crime!
Searching high, searching low,
A madman's chase, but what a show!

Incomplete Reflections of the Heart

I stare at the mirror, it stares back,
Where's the piece that fills my lack?
A smile here that's slightly askew,
Reflecting all the things I didn't pursue!

Oh, love's a game, but I'm missing dice,
Every moment held, but not so nice.
Chasing shadows, I tripped on my shoe,
And laughed at the mess I thought I knew.

A heart half-full's still pretty fun,
With jokes and jests on the run.
Who needs a full deck, anyway?
I'll play with futures, come what may!

With pieces scattered all around,
I gather smiles; that's my crown.
Reflection's puzzle, pieces askew,
But I'm still the artist; my heart's the glue!

Threads of Time Unraveled

Time unwinds like a silly string,
Got yarn in my hair—what a fling!
Pull a thread; watch it go,
This crazy ride's a burlesque show!

A tangle here, a twist there,
Weaving moments without a care.
Each stitch is a giggle, a wink of fate,
I laugh at my clock, a peculiar date!

Yesterday's snack, today's regret,
A blend of jitters and caffeinated fret.
Do I mend or leave it frayed?
A tapestry of blunders, well displayed!

As time dances, I join the fun,
Marching to the beat, never done.
Let the threads flap in the breeze,
For life's quirks are the greatest tease!

Shadows of What Might Be

I chased my shadow, it's a sly beast,
Teasing me, like a mischievous feast.
"Hey there, you," it whispers with glee,
"Catch me if you can, or just let it be!"

In the park, it dances on the grass,
I tried to catch it, but what a farce!
Laughing trees shake their leafy heads,
While squirrels plot how to fill our beds.

What could have been—a wild spree,
Days of sun, or sleep with tea.
Yet here I am, still trying to flee,
From shadows of what might never be.

Oh dear, it seems I'm quite the fool,
Running in circles, skipping school.
But here's to the dreams that often tease,
Let's twirl with shadows, if you please!

Unseen Connections

In a jigsaw box, I found a cow,
But it's missing a piece, oh, where art thou?
Cats and dogs dance, in the corner they leap,
While I'm puzzled and counting, can't find a sheep.

Noses in corners, and tails out of sight,
One sock from the laundry has taken a flight.
Bananas are laughing, how silly they seem,
Who knew fruit could tease, like a strange, twisted dream?

A rabbit with glasses can't see the way,
While I'm stuck here pondering over the fray.
A chicken crossed roads, but where would it go?
To find all the pieces? Oh, don't be so slow!

While marshmallows giggle in a pot of stew,
The answer's in sight, just not in my view.
With a spoon in one hand and a hat on my head,
I'm chasing the puzzle, wishing for bread.

The Journey of Discovery

A map half-finished, with crayons all bright,
Yelling, "We're lost!" but that's pure delight.
Raccoons in tuxedos waving, oh dear,
While I'm searching for paths that seem so unclear.

Footprints in pudding, a curious sight,
Alligators laughing, what gives them such might?
Unicorns prance in a field of pink grass,
While I'm laughing so hard, I near bust my glass.

The compass spins wildly, pizza slices fly,
My backpack's a monster that's eating some pie.
With jellybean maps leading me astray,
The journey's the giggle, come what may.

Tangled in taffy, I jump with a shout,
It's not just the edges; there's fun all about!
With confetti and laughter, oh what a climb,
Each twist and each turn makes wonderful rhyme.

Threads of Possibility

A yarn ball catastrophe, kittens take flight,
As I try to weave through this wild, funny night.
With spaghetti strands fuzzy and wavy, you see,
I'm knitting a scarf for a cat with a degree!

Bright ribbons of chaos, confoundingly bright,
Tangled together in a whimsy-filled night.
While popcorn's debating which string to entwine,
The colors are giggling, saying, "We're fine!"

Bubblegum visions and checkers that squawk,
Every thread is a story, not just idle talk.
A cat with old glasses scours for the clue,
In a tapestry town that's quite zany, it's true.

So bring on the fray, let's tie up the seams,
In the land of the loony, we dance with our dreams.
With snickers and chuckles, we wrap up this spree,
For each thread is a laughter, woven with glee.

The Missing Link in the Enigma

A sock in the dryer, a shoe on the street,
The mysteries grow with every misplaced feat.
I found half a sandwich under my bed,
Who knew I was hoarding my lunch well instead?

My keys play a game of hide and seek,
They thrive on confusion, oh what a sneak!
The more that I look, the better they hide,
In pockets of laughter, they waddle with pride.

Lost pens and old goals gather dust on the shelf,
Chasing my dreams while avoidin' myself.
It's chaos, it's funny, it's part of the show,
Perhaps this disarray is just how I grow!

A puzzle in pieces, a riddle in time,
Like trying to finish an unfinished rhyme.
So here's to the missing, the links we can't trace,
In this wild, silly dance called the human race.

Unfolding the Map of Existence

With crayons and laughter, I chart out my day,
A treasure map scribbled in a childlike way.
X marks the spot where I lost my shoe,
And Y leads to snacks, that's a clue I can chew!

I wander through mazes of cereal boxes,
Finding directions in all sorts of flopses.
A path made of giggles, with gigabytes too,
I think I might just get lost in my brew!

I check my GPS, it says I'm near,
But that's just a glitch—I mean, really, dear?
The road may be crooked, the signs may be worn,
But I'll laugh through my detours, till the break of dawn.

A map made of moments, I sketch out my quest,
With detours and snacks and a very nice rest.
I'll wander forever, come humor or rain,
In this goofy adventure, I'll never complain!

Glimpses of a Completed Canvas

A canvas of quirks sprawls wide on my floor,
With splashes of colors and mishaps galore.
My brush danced like a toddler ate cake,
And every rich hue was a laugh that I'd make.

Each stroke tells a story of things that went wrong,
Like a cat running wild through a fanciful song.
My masterpiece shouts with a chuckle or two,
It's ugly, it's funky, but oh how it's true!

Hidden behind all the chaos and mess,
Are moments of joy wrapped in all of this stress.
I glimpse my creations, the fun in each line,
Sipping on colors, I raise my glass of wine!

Beyond the mistakes, the picture unfolds,
In splashes of laughter, a tale to be told.
So here's to my canvas, my quirky delight,
In this world of errors, I'll shine out so bright!

The Art of Embracing the Unknown

In the realm of question marks, I take a stroll,
With humor in hand, oh it makes me feel whole.
What's the worst that could happen, I think with a grin,
I might just uncover a fantastic win!

A missing left shoe and an upside-down hat,
Create fashion statements, just imagine that!
I stroll through this party of unplanned events,
While laughter erupts at my fashion's expense.

Each twist of the plot is a giggle I crave,
Like dancing through life not knowing the wave.
I'm twirling through chaos with style and flair,
Embracing the wild without any care.

So pass me confusion, please pour on the jokes,
With every surprise that my heart gently pokes.
In the art of unknown, I find all my cheer,
For in every odd moment, adventure is near!

The Unraveled Narrative

In a box marked 'lost', I found a sock,
A jigsaw piece playing hide and seek in a dock,
With every twist and turn, I laugh and scoff,
Wondering if even the cat's plan is a spoof.

Coffee stains map out a story untold,
A spoon's a hero in the land of the bold,
Each random crumb feels like fortune, behold!
And the milk jug? A sidekick of pure gold.

The remote's missing, where could it be?
Behind the couch or lost in the sea?
Sometimes the banter of toys is a spree,
As the dog tries to share his secret decree.

In this maze of chaos, fun comes alive,
Like a dinner without forks, we just dive,
Each laugh we uncover, we joyfully strive,
In the absurd, who knows what we'll derive!

Discovering the Missing Elements

Lost the keys while searching for lunch,
A sandwich that smells like an old monkey's punch,
Questing for snacks—oh, what a hunch,
In a treasure map of crumbs, I start to munch.

A cactus in the center of my chaotic den,
Where did the cat hide my favorite pen?
Every object is a riddle, again and again,
Is this life's way of giving me zen?

Each blender blade spins like my thoughts,
While my shoe's lost somewhere in the knots,
The toaster's a joker, making toast that's caught,
In this whimsical dance of life's silly plots.

The puzzles we solve could fill a book,
With a dash of whimsy and a funny nook,
In the chaos we dance, let's take a look,
Between the missing elements, laughter's the hook!

Charting the Uncharted

With a map on napkins, I scribble my dreams,
Where spaghetti dots line up with whipped cream,
In the realm of nonsense, it's never as it seems,
A rubber chicken sails in outrageous streams.

An envelope marked "Return to Sender,"
Holds the prize of a sushi blender,
The GPS laughs, it's a master pretender,
Routing me through the world of a vendor.

In the land where socks and spoons unite,
I wander through whimsy, a curious sight,
Each step I take, a new dimensional light,
A treasure hunt beckons late into the night.

Through the trails of confusion, joy takes flight,
Navigating chaos, always feels right,
With every twist, and each twisty bite,
Charting the uncharted, pure delight!

Conversations with the Undefined

Banana peels tell tales in a slippery way,
While coffee mugs giggle at my dismay,
A diary speaks of a cake gone astray,
In whispers of cookies, they start to play.

The clock chimes 13, it's lost its routine,
As socks swap opinions on colors unseen,
Where's the lost puzzle? It's never been keen,
In the anxious chatter of creatures pristine.

If a broom could talk, oh what tales it would spin,
Of dust bunnies plotting their grand win,
In the corners of rooms, they quietly grin,
Laughing at chaos where it all begins.

Whimsical chats fill the air with a jest,
Each moment of silliness becomes the best,
Through undefined corners, we stumble and quest,
Finding the beauty in madness, a joyful fest!

Reflections in a Shattered Mirror

In a mirror cracked, my hair's a fright,
Thought I saw wisdom, but it gave me a fright.
I smiled at the shards, they laughed right back,
Whispers of chaos echo through the crack.

My socks aren't matched, it's a fashion faux pas,
Yet I strut like a peacock, with flair and a draw.
Who needs a plan when you can just wing?
Nature's odd jigsaw gives life a good zing.

Chicken dances bring all the fun to the brunch,
Fried eggs on the plate are the start of a munch.
The toast burned nicely, it's burnt char and cheer,
Reflections in chaos, oh, what a career!

Harmony Found in Disarray

The laundry basket sings, a colorful song,
Mismatched socks dance, they can't get along.
Faded shirts tell tales of spaghetti spills,
While dust bunnies boast of their mountain-like thrills.

The cat's on the curtain; the dog's in a chair,
A circus of critters, oh, life isn't fair!
Yet streaming laughter from the living room flows,
In the chaos of home, true harmony grows.

The fridge has a party, leftovers galore,
Vying for attention, they demand to explore.
With spoons as the symphony, they all take the stage,
In disarray we find a beautiful page.

Capturing Shadows of Potential

A shadow duck waddles across the bright floor,
Sketching wild dreams like paper galore.
With crayons of optimism, I doodle my fate,
Each line draws a giggle, not a worry or weight.

Our plans may be foggy, like a mystery book,
Yet we paint with broad strokes, just take a look.
The spilled juice splashes; it's art in a cup,
With every small failure, I'm ready to sup.

Caught in the sunlight, the dust dances high,
Reflecting bright futures that twirl in the sky.
Each fragment a mirage, each moment a chance,
In capturing shadows, let's join in the dance.

The Search for Wholeness Amidst the Fragments

In the garden of mishaps, I plant my dread,
Pants with holes tell stories of fun I misled.
Yet weeds hold their ground, and daisies stand tall,
Fractured and odd, we're having a ball.

Lost puzzle pieces under the couch lie in wait,
Searching for edges, but I find an old plate.
I chuckle and ponder, is this my new art?
A mix of the lost and the found plays its part.

My mug says 'you're special' with one tiny chip,
Yet it holds all my secrets, my hopes and my sip.
Together we gather the shards of each day,
In the search for wholeness, we laugh on our way!

Bittersweet Echoes of Abandonment

Left my socks in the dryer, they roam,
Lost in a land far from home.
Where do the mismatched wander, I ask,
The ultimate quest, too much to bask.

A lone spoon hides within the pan,
Making mischief, it began to plan.
The toaster snickers, the blender laughs,
In this wild kitchen, we're all daft.

Every missed piece tells a tale,
Like when my sandwich learned to sail.
With peanut butter, it took to the breeze,
Now I'm hoping for lunch, not a tease.

The socks may find a friend or two,
In the realm of the lost and the blue.
A hilarious dance on the floor,
As they echo the laughter, forevermore.

A Portrait of Variable Stories

A cat in a hat, what a sight to see,
Sipping on tea with a bumblebee.
The squirrel sculpts tales from pine,
While fish plan a heist, looking so fine.

In the gallery of time, clocks stand still,
As shadows play games, what a thrill!
The frames are crooked, but who would care,
When every odd piece brings laughter to air.

A rabbit with shoes that are two sizes wide,
Dances through stories, a wobbly guide.
Each stride brings giggles, pure bliss,
In this madcap gallery, who could resist?

The artist chuckles at the frame's embrace,
As the whims of his brush leave no trace.
A portrait of moments, both quirky and bright,
Each brushstroke tells tales in the dim light.

Upon the Stretched Strings of Fate

A cat plays tunes, much to my surprise,
With a fiddle that's made of my old ties.
The dog joins in, howls like a pro,
Making me laugh till my sides overflow.

The goldfish sways, a dancer so bold,
While the parrot squawks stories untold.
Together they mix a peculiar blend,
I'm stuck in their show; I can't pretend.

Marbles roll across the creaky floor,
They chat with the dust bunnies, what a chore!
"Keep it together," I mumble with glee,
In this circus of antics, they're wild and free.

Yet among all the chaos, there's a tune,
A harmony birthed beneath the moon.
Strings may be stretched, but the laughter stays,
In this whimsical world where hilarity plays.

The Search for Clarity in Confusion

A map of chocolate crumbs on the run,
Leading to nowhere, oh what fun!
Each twist and turn is a candy caper,
With gummy bears as my next paper.

I tried to ask a squirrel for tips,
It just stared back, not moving its lips.
So, I ventured onward, a brave little soul,
Through forests of fluff, chasing my goal.

The trees are gossiping, I swear it's true,
Every leaf has a tale, and a wry view.
"Clarity's here, just look down below,"
But all I see is a lovely potato.

In the wiggly path of the jumbled mess,
Each bump brings laughter; I must confess.
So here I remain, with a grin on my face,
Lost in confusion, but enjoying the chase.

The Symphony of the Unfinished

In a world where socks go missing,
The orchestra of chaos sings.
With mismatched shoes on my feet,
I two-step to the beat of springs.

Oh, look there's not one but three cats!
They're composing a meow for the show.
While I search for my car keys,
They're plotting their cute little overthrow.

Notes scatter like crumbs on the floor,
A melody of laughter fills the air.
When I finally get my tune right,
The fridge is empty, but I don't care!

So here's to the tunes left unsung,
And the dance of the perfectly wrong.
For in every missed note and slip,
Life's strange rhythm plays along!

Dreams on the Fringes

I dreamt I was a superhero,
With a cape made of duct tape.
But I stumbled on my own feet,
And fell with a cartoonish scrape.

My powers were quite absurd,
Turning coffee into a pie.
But when I tried to fly high,
I just ended up asking why?

From the rooftop, I took my leap,
Expecting grace and flair.
Instead, I landed in the trash,
And now it's my throne, I swear!

So here's my toast to dreams bizarre,
Where I'm never quite the king.
It's the wild whimsy of my night,
That keeps me inventing!

Unfolding the Hidden Narrative

Every drawer has secrets untold,
In a land of old shoes and pens.
I'm searching for the plot in this mess,
While my lost thoughts play with hens!

I found a note from a birthday past,
On a cake that was never baked.
It said, "Keep laughing, and don't look back!"
So I chuckled as my plans flaked.

The chapters jump like a wild jackrabbit,
Telling tales in bits and bobs.
I'm living in a sitcom, I swear,
With punchlines from the jobs!

So here's to narratives that twist,
With characters made of giggles.
For every hidden plot and twist,
Turns my life into endless wiggles!

The Dance of Fragmented Moments

In the kitchen, I'm a chef so bold,
With a recipe written in crayon.
I dance between the pots and plates,
While juggling waffles like a swan.

A splash of joy, a sprinkle of glee,
The blender's now part of the fun.
But when it bursts like a comedy,
I'm left with a pancake run!

At the park, my picnic's a sight,
With sandwiches that look like art.
But we forgot the ants at the fight,
Now I'm dining with a tiny heart.

So here's to the moments that break,
In dances as odd as a jive!
For in all the fragments we make,
Is the joy of feeling alive!

Distorted Realities and Unseen Patterns

In a world where socks go to hide,
And mismatched pairs are worn with pride.
I search for the corner of my lost mind,
While everyday logic has gone blind.

The cat rules the house, not a single doubt,
As I navigate bright socks and trails of grout.
The fridge hums secrets of leftovers past,
But who knew the weirdness would happen so fast?

Puzzles are scattered, scattered with flair,
The dog chewed the edges, but I don't care.
Every twisted piece, a laugh to unfurl,
In a meddled-up chaos, we dance and twirl.

The clock ticks wildly, yet it feels quite right,
As I ration my snacks like they're hidden in sight.
With sarcasm sharp and a smile so wide,
The edges of sanity we take in stride.

Constellations of Untold Journeys

In a galaxy full of lost keys,
I drift in a cosmos of mismatched tease.
I swear I parked right by the moon,
But somehow found Mars in the afternoon.

My luggage wanders through space and time,
To places unknown, it reasons to climb.
While I sip coffee in a black hole's spin,
Missing the flight I thought I'd been in.

Planets collide, chaos in flight,
Yet we laugh at the stars on a silly bright night.
Chasing comets with shoes tied in loops,
The universe giggles at our clumsy scoops.

So we'll toast with gravity, it's quite absurd,
To journeys misplanned and memories blurred.
Each trip a new riddle, each tale a delight,
As we wander 'neath constellations that ignite.

The Balance of Connection and Disconnection

Two friends texting from totally strange lands,
Sending emojis that nobody understands.
In a world of devices, we laugh and we sigh,
As Wi-Fi reminds us that we still need to try.

In a restaurant full of screens and clicks,
We're glued to our phones, missing the tricks.
Yet we share a wink, an unplugged embrace,
While our desserts arrive at a snail's pace.

A group gathering, laughter fills the air,
Yet every head bobs in a digital stare.
With virtual hearts helping us connect,
While real hugs feel like ancient relics to respect.

So let's balance our pixels with moments of glee,
As we joke about how strange we can be.
For in the disconnection, we still find a thread,
A funny old bond, 'tis enough said.

Fragments of Existence

With crumbs in the corners, a life quite whimsical,
I ponder the meaning of crumbs being chemical.
My coffee spills stories that nobody knows,
As I dodge my own thoughts like a game of low blows.

Jigsaw pieces scattered near and far,
Glimpse a weird world like a drinking bazaar.
The cat stares in judgment, that furry sage,
While I squeeze my chaos into a page.

Each wrinkle and glitch, a mark of the show,
As I juggle my fears like a circus, you know.
In tune with the whimsy of mismatched delight,
I gather the fragments, oh what a sight!

So here's to the moments that don't quite align,
With laughter and nonsense, we dance out of line.
For in this confusion, it starts to make sense,
A riddle of joy, our own recompense.

Unraveled Threads of Time

In a world where socks go to hide,
Mismatched pairs are my daily pride.
I search for the answers in laundry piles,
But they all just giggle in rainbow styles.

The clock is ticking, yet it seems quite slow,
I trip over time like it's a rubber toe.
Each tick a puzzle, a riddle it sends,
I laugh at the chaos that never quite ends.

Yet in the chaos, pieces emerge,
A glimpse of the picture begins to surge.
I might be late, but who needs a plan?
I dance through confusion like a wobbly man.

Time's threads are tangled, but that's just fine,
I'll toast to confusion with a glass of wine.
For every odd moment is a chance to tease,
Life's quirks are the joys that aim to please!

Beyond the Frame of Understanding

I bought a frame for my perfect art,
But instead, it just showcased a cat with a fart.
The picture's askew, but I think that's the aim,
It adds to the charm, and who's to blame?

Brushstrokes of laughter fill in the gaps,
Where logic escaped and sanity naps.
I swing through the chaos with colors so bright,
Creating a canvas of pure delight.

What's normal or strange? It's all just a giggle,
I scribble my thoughts, give my pencil a wiggle.
Each crooked attempt is a laugh shared with fate,
In the frame of confusion, I'll happily wait.

So here's to the mess, let it flourish and grow,
For beyond the frame is where the fun flows.
In the abstract expanse where we all might stray,
I'll dance with the weirdness—come what may!

The Questions Between Moments

What's this sandwich that's falling apart?
Is it the mayo or just my bad art?
Each bite is a mystery wrapped in a crust,
I chew on the questions, it's a must.

Why are there always more crumbs than cheese?
Do toasters conspire, do they do it to tease?
Each breakfast a riddle, a giggle in bread,
Life's tasty mess, and it's filling my head.

In the gap between moments, chaos prevails,
The bread might get soggy, but laughter never fails.
So I raise my toast, all cheers and delight,
For the questions we ask in our random bites.

It's not about answers, or what we unearth,
It's the joy in the journey, the laughter, the mirth.
If sandwiches giggle, then so will I,
With crumbs on my shirt, and laughter nearby!

Embracing Imperfections

Oh, the art of a cake that leans to one side,
It's not a disaster; it's a roller-coaster ride.
With sprinkles that tumble and frosting that drips,
It's a masterpiece born of sweet little blips.

My crooked little lines on the canvas of dreams,
Are just happy accidents, or so it seems.
Each brushstroke a giggle, each dab a delight,
In the mess of creation, it all feels just right.

A symphony played on untuned guitar,
Brings a song full of heart, wonder, and bizarre.
We dance to the rhythm, imperfect yet real,
For laughter's the music that helps us to heal.

So here's to the flaws that make us unique,
In every misstep, it's joy that we seek.
Life's funny little quirks make us shine from within,
Embracing the imperfect, let the fun begin!

The Search for Wholeness

I searched high and low, oh what a quest,
To find my lost pieces and feel my best.
One sock is missing, where did it go?
Perhaps with my keys that lost all their glow.

I gathered my thoughts, my plans were laid,
Only to find my calendar was frayed.
Dinner's at six, but what's on the plate?
A mystery wrapped in an old paper crate.

I asked my goldfish, he gave me a stare,
While spinning in circles, unaware of my despair.
With each twist and turn, I chuckled aloud,
Is this the whole me? I'm surely quite proud!

So here I stand, a jigsaw of glee,
Embracing the quirks that make up me.
In laughter I find, though pieces are few,
The search for wholeness is a silly debut.

Navigating the Unknown Terrain

With maps upside down, I'm lost in the wood,
Pine trees are pointing, but none understood.
I thought I'd see bears, instead just a bee,
Buzzing around me like it's just here to tease.

I tripped on a root, did a comical dance,
While branches were tugging at my pants.
A squirrel threw acorns as if to say,
'Keep going, my friend, you'll find your way!'

By streams I meander, with ducks on parade,
Charting my course through the leafy cascade.
But who needs a map when you're this much fun?
I'll just follow the sun till the day is done.

With laughter my compass, I wander and roam,
Making each wrong turn lead me back home.
The unknown terrain is a sight to behold,
As the stories unfold, adventures unfold.

Incomplete Journeys

On a train to nowhere, I sat with my snack,
A ticket to dreams, but they all lack.
The scenery whirls like a whirlwind of fun,
Each stop is a giggle, but I'm not quite done.

I packed up my hopes, left some in the rain,
A collection of wishes, like bubbles of pain.
But with every misstep, I learn how to hop,
Embracing my quirks, I refuse to stop.

Stumbling on paths that twist and they turn,
I weave through the tangle, oh how I've learned!
Incomplete my journey, like a half-done pie,
Yet sweetness abounds as I laugh and I try.

With every bump taken, every wrong track,
Comes a lesson in joy, never looking back.
Embracing the whimsy of journeys askew,
I find that in fragments, I'm whole and anew.

Weaving Dreams from Shadows

With shadows as threads under moonlight's glow,
I stitch up my dreams, in fabric they flow.
A patchwork of wishes, some bright, some quite bleak,
Each snip of the scissors brings laughter to speak.

In corners I glimpse the fears that entwine,
Yet they dance like confetti, as sweet as a wine.
I gather the moments like stars in a net,
Each one's a giggle I never forget.

Laughter surrounds me, a shimmering veil,
As I butterfly flip through an impossible tale.
The cloth of my thoughts is a riotous mix,
Stitched up with love, and a few silly tricks.

With shadows as colors and dreams as my thread,
I weave my own journey, where no path is led.
Embracing the chaos, it all seems so bright,
In this tapestry of shadows, I dance with delight.

Through a Kaleidoscope of Choices

Spin the wheel, let's start anew,
Pick a color, any hue!
Red for coffee, green for tea,
One more sip and we'll agree.

Twist in circles, dance around,
Every option is so profound!
A square peg in a round hole,
Just grab a snack, that's the goal!

Tangled paths that lead to fun,
Choose your shortcut, just for one.
Tickle the edges, tease the frame,
In this game, we're all the same!

So why not laugh at each wrong turn?
There's much to gain, so much to learn.
With giggles echoing through the air,
Let's celebrate the whimsy there!

When All the Colors Don't Align

Paint your world with shades of wrong,
Where pink and green don't quite belong.
A purple sky, a yellow sun,
In this artwork, does it run?

Stripes and polka dots in pairs,
Clashing clothes and wild new flares.
Walking on rainbows, tripping too,
Now that's a magical view!

An orange cat on blue grass lies,
Confused yet charming in our eyes.
Colors scream out, 'What is this?'
A laughter here, you can't resist!

So let's embrace the wild and weird,
Cheer for chaos, let humor be cheered.
With mismatched edges we'll align,
Together we'll drink confusion as wine!

Tracing the Edges of Possibility

With crayons drawn on foggy glass,
We sketch our dreams and let them pass.
Around the edges, doubts abound,
But funny shapes are what we've found.

Tracing lines like a curious kid,
Where did I slip? Where did I skid?
A puppy barks, and off we go,
Chasing trails of what we know.

We stumble not, but weave a tale,
Every fail's a funny scale.
Wobbly curves and wild designs,
Oh, how the laughter brightly shines!

Let's cheer for quirks that make us whole,
In every fumble, find the soul.
With each odd edge we twist and turn,
In every wacky space, we learn!

Navigating the Maze of the Self

In a maze that spins with every choice,
Doesn't it make you question your voice?
Two paths fork, a squirrel's the guide,
Nuts of wisdom, I can't decide!

Left takes me to the land of snack,
Right leads to wisdom, what do I lack?
But hey, a donut's good for thought,
Two bites in, and wisdom's sought!

How do we wander in such delight?
Each wrong turn feels so very right.
Even the walls have silly pranks,
So much joy in misfit ranks!

With laughter echoing through the maze,
Who knew confusion could amaze?
Embrace the twists, don't walk in line,
For it's the funny paths that shine!

Aligning the Disparate

One sock's bright, the other's dull,
Yet in my drawer, they sit full.
A puzzle made of mismatched flair,
A runway show of what to wear.

The cat thinks it's a game to hide,
Under the couch, there's nowhere to hide.
While I chase its tail and sneak,
I wonder whose joy feels less bleak?

A spoon with a fork? Quite the debate!
Who knew cutlery's love life was fate?
In the kitchen, we dance and spin,
With plates and cups that all have a grin.

So here's my jigsaw, silly and bright,
With quirky corners, it's pure delight.
Who cares if the edges don't quite align?
It's all just part of the fun, divine!

The Labyrinth of Choices

At breakfast, I ponder the cereal aisle,
Do I want a crunch, or a flakes-style?
The golden box whispers my name,
But the colorful one sings just the same.

To tie my shoes or wear those slides?
This decision feels like high tides.
Should I go out, or stay right in?
The couch seems snug, with that old rerun din.

Shall I wear stripes, or stick with polka dots?
The mirror holds secrets, it laughs and taunts.
Picking outfits feels like a quest,
Who knew fashion could feel like a test?

In this maze of choices, I feel quite bold,
Who knew life came with a wardrobe of gold?
With every turn, a laugh to find,
I'll wear mismatched socks, and peace of mind!

Tapestries of Experience

Grandma's quilt made of hopes and threads,
Each stich a tale, like sweet little spreads.
A patch from my trip to the fair,
With a pocket for gum, and memories to share.

There's a piece from the cat's little heist,
When it stole my lunch, oh what a tryst!
A tapestry woven with laughter and care,
Gifts from the past, with a pinch of flair.

Stains of ice cream, and spills of tea,
Each mark a memory, as wild as can be.
I'll add more patches, the future's still bright,
With every misstep, I'll gather delight.

So let's stitch together this colorful spree,
With love and with laughter, just you wait and see.
For every quirky thread has its place,
In the grand quilt of this wonderful space!

Threads of Tomorrow

With twine in hand, I spin my fate,
A web of decisions—I can't be late!
Should I start with a dance or just relax?
At each new dawn, I'll choose to unwind my tracks.

Yesterday's yarn is tangled and frayed,
But tomorrow's threads are waiting, displayed.
Shall I go for the wild colors, oh so bold?
Or stick with the past, quite cozy and old?

The future's a tapestry waiting to grow,
I'll weave in some laughter and let the sun glow.
With threads of ambition, and needles of cheer,
I'll sew a bright future, stitched with no fear.

So here's to tomorrow, so fun and so new,
With bright colored fibers, and joy to imbue.
As I thread my way to where I belong,
In the rhythm of life, I'll sing my own song!

Gathering the Fragments

I woke up today, pieces in sight,
Scattered around, oh what a fright!
The cat's on my lap, my coffee's amiss,
Searching for edges, I start with a kiss.

Jigsaw puzzles tease, like socks in the wash,
Where'd they all go? It feels like a squash!
Terrible angles and colors that clash,
But hey, it's a game, so we'll make a splash!

The dog wants my focus, the kids make a mess,
Can't find the border; life's such a chess!
I stack up the pieces, a tower of fun,
Won't stop till I finish, and maybe once run!

So here I sit, fragments in hand,
Realizing maybe I'll never understand.
But laughter surrounds, and that's just the key,
With jumbled-up pieces, I'm still quite happy!

The Beauty of Incompletion

Half a sock here, a shoe over there,
A sandwich for lunch, and crumbs everywhere.
I'm building a tower of stuff that won't fit,
Incompletion's beauty, a perfect misfit!

The dishes are dirty, the laundry's a chore,
I bake a small cake, but forget the core.
Life's little messes all seem so absurd,
Like Frank's new hairstyle – a flock of wild birds!

Scattered ideas, from here to the moon,
Still trying to find that elusive tune.
A dance in the chaos, a laugh in the storm,
Bring on the quirks, they're the real norm!

Maybe perfection is just way too bland,
Let's embrace the weird, take a stand.
Incompletion's charm, a rather fine art,
A landscape of laughter, a tapestry of heart!

Sifting Through Uncertainty

When the fridge is empty, and I can't decide,
Do I make a sandwich or just take a ride?
The clock keeps on ticking, the day gets more loud,
Sifting through choices, it's like wading through crowds!

The socks keep on vanishing, a puzzle profound,
One's striped and the other? Has left town,
I'm not really sure if I'm winning or lost,
Wait, did I order lunch? Oh, what's the cost?

My thoughts swirl like spaghetti, all twirled up in chaos,
With options like candy, but none that get payoffs.
I wait for an answer, but the sky's still blue,
Turns out uncertainty just wants to chew!

But hey, it's a party, even if it's unclear,
Grab all the snacks, let's drown all the fear.
With laughter as glue, and confusion as spice,
Here's to uncertainty, oh, isn't it nice?

Fractals of the Heart

In a world full of shapes, I find my own way,
A circle of friends, and a heart that can play.
But wait, there's a triangle stuck in my shoe,
Fractals of love, they're silly but true!

My heart's like a puzzle, with pieces that frown,
Who knew a good laugh could turn it around?
We spin in the chaos, like tops made of fun,
While counting the edges 'til we all come undone!

Patterns of joy and shade, oh what a blend,
In laughter we twirl, with no need to pretend.
Unraveled and tangled, just how we are,
Dancing through fractals, we shine like a star!

Through heart-shaped mazes and love's little quirks,
We chase every giggle, and it totally works.
So here's to our journey, messy yet smart,
In this fractal adventure, we're never apart!

www.ingramcontent.com/pod-product-compliance
Lightning Source LLC
Chambersburg PA
CBHW051656160426
43209CB00004B/917